Why *Not* Socialism

*Against G.A. Cohen's defence of
socialism's feasibility and desirability*

Igor Caldeira

Title: *Why* Not *Socialism - Against G.A. Cohen's defence of socialism's feasibility and desirability*

Author: Igor Caldeira

ID: 14021501

ISBN: 978-1-291-51502-2

Category: Human Sciences

Publisher: Lulu

Copyright: Igor Caldeira, © 2013

Language: English

Country: Belgium

Keywords: G. A. Cohen, egalitarianism, democratic planning, economic democracy, socialism, market, Marx, Hayek, Mises, analytic philosophy

License: Standard Copyright License

The present work was developed with the support of *Fundação para a Ciência e Tecnologia* (Research Scholarship SFRH/BD/61238/2009), financed through POPH-QREN – Tyopology 4.1, co-funded by the European Social Fund and Portuguese resources from MCTES.

Abstract: In his last book, *Why Not Socialism?*, Gerald Allan Cohen uses as a departure point for his argument in favour of a democratic non-market economic system the example of a camping trip.

In it, the author states, most people will intuitively accept as normal an egalitarian principle of organization with common property over all goods.

In this essay, we intend to show several problems with the book.

First, that we must try several possible situations with distinct characteristics, and see if the same organisational solutions emerge, or if our intuitions lead us in other ways.

Second, we intend to prove that indeed our intuitions about how human groups should organise themselves in different circumstances will lead us in different directions depending on the context.

Third, that the moral issue is not to be dismissed as easily as Cohen does in favour of technical considerations and that democracy - which is essentially a mechanism that is inspired by some values and not a value in itself - cannot be used as an argument to defend economic planning.

Keywords: G. A. Cohen, egalitarianism, democratic planning, economic democracy, socialism, market

Index

Introduction

In *Why Not Socialism?* Gerald Allan Cohen reaffirms his support for a socialist society based upon a purely non-market economic system, using for such an example (a camping trip) that, he believes, can be transposed into our societies, provided we develop the adequate social technologies.

This small but challenging book, with its inspiring camping trip case, has already been object of many reviews, and some in-depth articles. Among them, I would mention Richard W. Miller (2010), John E. Roemer (2010) and Jason Brennan (2012).

As we shall see, it is here done a critique in similar lines to those of Brennan, but with a different methodology and in fact criticizing the idea of democracy, a concept that is used by Cohen as some kind of magic word to purify and justify economic planning. We will here attempt to show that there are several, both analytical and moral issues that the book fails to answer. Does a camping trip example respond both to the moral and the technical problems of cooperation in society? Do we find in the camping trip the desirable moral sentiments for big societies? And if morally desirable, are they possible? Can we have something like a decentralized, non-authoritarian economic planning system? Is *democratic* economic planning (that Cohen defends) in any way different than a centralized economic planning system? Finally: does a democratic economic planning respect Cohen's premises on moral and anthropological issues?

Such premises are three: first, that *personal choices are morally relevant*; second, that *people being free to make those choices* is also relevant; and third, *Cohen does not have a negative anthropological perspective* (people are not ontologically bad according to him; a pessimist look on human ontology would justify authoritarian solutions, and the author overtly rejects authoritarianism).

Regarding the first premise, Cohen believes it is relevant that "people care about, and, where necessary and possible, for, one another, and, too, care that they care about one another" (Cohen, 2009, pp.34/35).

Regarding the second premise, Cohen writes in the last page of the book that "Every market, even a socialist market, is a system of predation" (p.82). So, even market socialism is unacceptable to Cohen. But he also states that in his camping trip example "the right to personal choice can be exercised, without strain, consistently with equality and community" (

p.76). His challenge is having a non-market system where preferences can be freely exercised.

Regarding the third premise, Cohen does not think that human beings are essentially bad: the failure of socialism, in his opinion, is more due to the "lack of a suitable organizational technology" than to "human selfishness" (p.58).

In the first section of this essay we will explain Cohen's arguments. Which are his basic principles? What does Cohen mean with "desirability" and "feasibility" of the socialist project? Why does he reject any kind of market (even market socialism)? How can we know what does he intend to defend?

In the second section we will approach the technical and analytical underpinnings of the discussion surrounding the organization of human groups. Since Cohen affirms this (the *technical*) is the main issue, we will dedicate most of our attention to it, developing our refutation in three steps. First, we will create a framework to evaluate groups. Second, we want to know which dimensions can be used to understand the interaction between individuals. Plus, we also want to know which basic structures of group organization can there be. And third, we will evaluate several possible types of group; the first will be Cohen's camping trip. Departing from such example, we will think of other situations. Which are the similarities and which are the disparities among them?

In the third section we will show that if (and only if) we are really committed to the three assumptions (moral relevance of choices, freedom of choice and belief in human goodness) previously described, an economic system following Cohen's principles of equality and community are not feasible in certain types of situations/ groups, or at the very least that he, with his example, did not manage to bring us any closer to understand how economic planning is anything other than, at best, *just* centralized and, at worst, plainly authoritarian.

The problem, contrary to what Cohen states, is not only that a total economic planning is technically catastrophic within our present state of knowledge, but also, and more fundamentally when we talk of large human groups, because it creates a contradiction between the advocated assumptions on moral beings and the results of centralized decision making. In the end, we here state, there is, at heart, no difference between Cohen's "democratic" planning and an authoritarian planning, and we also affirm that that contradiction derives above all from his principle of community.

I - Cohen's argument explained

Literature review

Miller (2010) does an analysis of both Cohen's luck egalitarianism and Rawls' original position, pointing their flaws. He also poses the problems of convictions/ideals and the impact of our (political) choices on others.

Roemer (2010) denies Cohen's assertion that the main problem is one of design (how to make socialism work) and also that market, assisted by pervasive social welfare, is enough to produce socialism. The question for Roemer is how to get there, his answer being that "depressions and major wars" tend to generate the needed dissemination and equalization of risks throughout the whole society, instead of, like in normal circumstances, leaving it only to the poorer, less fortunate layers of society (Roemer, 2010, p.262).

Brennan, from a different perspective, states, like Roemer, that Cohen is wrong in thinking that greed and fear are intrinsic to market economy. And, like Miller (but in a more straightforward way) he also says that we cannot compare an ideal society (so, ideal socialism) with a real society (so, real capitalism) like Cohen actually does. We can only compare ideals with ideals (as a model of an ideal capitalist society, he presents Ayn Rand's "Galt's Gutch", from her book *Atlas Shrugged*) and real societies with real societies (so effective socialism with effective capitalism). Brennan applies Cohen methodology to show its flaws; but instead of attacking capitalism from a socialist perspective, he attacks democracy from an anarchist one. The conclusion is that of course that the anarchist ideal seems much more appealing than the democratic reality we live in - but it does not mean that democracy is bad. It is the best we have *to live in*.

Cohen's argument explained

The camping trip example

Cohen presents us an example: a camping trip, in which several people, with different skills, go together and cooperate. With it he intends to show that in some contexts "most people, even most *anti*egalitarians" prefer to have a cooperation in which "everybody has a roughly similar opportunity to flourish, and also to relax, on condition that she contributes, appropriately to her capacity, to the flourishing and relaxing of others." (2009, pp.4/5). At the same time, he accepts that there are many differences between a camping trip and society, and that the task, for a socialist, is understanding "precisely what are the differences that matter and how can [they] address them" (p.11). This question is never answered across the book. The only references to the differences between the camping trip and normal life in society are to the fact that the camping trip is limited in time, gathers a small amount of people and happens in a "happy recreational context" (on pages 53/54 for example), and this only to dismiss those differences without explaining why.

The egalitarian principle

The first principle explained by Cohen and that, according to him, is present in the camping trip example, is the egalitarian principle. He develops this principle as an "equality of opportunity" principle, which may present itself in three distinct interpretations: the *bourgeois*, the *left-liberal* and the *radical* or *socialist*.

The bourgeois principle of equality of opportunity is essentially formal and removes those social and/or legal restraints to the flourishing of individuals based on status (for example, social class, gender or race). The left-liberal principle goes further on the social aspect and focuses on allowing that success be determined more by talents than social origin; such is the aim of free and mandatory education, for example.

Finally, the egalitarian principle endorsed by Cohen is the radical one, which intends to correct all disadvantages that were not chosen by individuals.

This socialist equality of opportunity is nevertheless consistent with three forms of inequality. It allows disadvantages resulting from choices regarding, for example, trade-offs between leisure and work. This first principle results from the *variety of preferences* and lifestyle choices and is consistent with the socialist principle because people have chosen to work more or have more leisure, and don't regret their choice. The second form, which Cohen designates as *regrettable choice*, poses more problems because although it is essentially equal to the first, in this second an actor regrets the choice made, thinking he would have been better off had he made other choice. The third form of inequality is the *option luck*, in which absolute equality of opportunities lead to an unequal result.

The two latter forms of inequality of results do not fit into the socialist ideal, although they are allowed by the socialist principle of equality of opportunity. Multiplied across a large society they produce large inequalities; to counter them, Cohen presents a second principle.

The principle of community

This is the principle that Cohen uses to support a situation of absolute equality. Inequalities, while allowed by the socialist principle of equality of opportunities, destroy the feeling of community by separating people regarding material goods. Large inequalities separate people from one another. This principle requires that "people care about, and, where necessary and possible, for, one another, and, too, care that they care about one another" (pp.34/35).

So, we conclude, mere redistribution policies are not sufficient. Using the State to correct inequalities is just one part of the issue. The main part is that people must "care that they care". It is not only a matter of political economy; it is a matter of morality. The socialist ethos according to the author requires redistribution to be voluntary. It is morally relevant that people adhere to "[c]ommunal reciprocity [which] is the antimarket principle" based on a "commitment to one's fellow human beings [and not] on the basis of cash reward" (p.39).

So, and as we have said before, personal choices are morally relevant in Cohen: the mere political imposition of a "cooperative" scheme is not enough.

Desirability and Feasibility

Moral desirability

Cohen's argument regarding the moral desirability can be resumed in the idea "that all people of goodwill would welcome the news that it had become possible" to base the economic system on generosity towards everyone else; that generosity was not only limited to the small groups and those who are closer to us; and that the market, which is only possible through self-interest, had thus disappeared.

Of course that saying that someone who does not support such idea is automatically ill-intentioned does put some stress on possible answers. But two objections may nevertheless be raised to Cohen's perspective; the first is the *psychological limits* of human beings, and does not properly address Cohen's objection; the second is the *moral dimension of the market*, and is only partly suitable to provide such answer.

Regarding the psychological limits, it is yet to be proven that human beings can actually maintain a high level of care for others, for actually everybody, as if they were our parents, or our brothers or sisters, or our sons or daughters, or our close friends. Not only is it unlikely that we can feel the same (caring) way for everybody equally, regardless of their relation towards us, but more importantly it is highly doubtful that we can maintain a constant level of emotional excitement, of love, towards others (and this without necessarily being selfish). But to this Cohen might object that if we are not capable of deeply caring on a constant level for everyone else on the planet, we just are not people of goodwill.

So we may raise the second objection. Cohen is naturally right that the market is an efficient system of transformation of the basic instinct of self-interest to the profit of society. But he fails to see that the market is not all about selfishness. In a market system no one is entirely selfish, or exclusively selfish. There are some rules, and the respect of such rules includes a respect for others as well. In fact, the respect of rules may be entirely unselfish because when we accept them we also have to accept that in some cases we will lose. We will have to accept that sometimes all parties will win, in others we will win - and in other times we will lose. Selfish people might accept that other people could win *if* they themselves could also win - but they would never accept losing. This second objection might provide a better answer for Cohen because it does include a universal duty of caring - but again, the author can object that the *deep reason* for this acceptance of rules of conduct that sometimes will benefit us and sometimes not is not that we care for one another, and we care that we care, but only because we care for ourselves enough to know that, overall, the market works better for all, and thus also for us. Even not being only about selfishness, the market will always include selfishness.

Technical feasibility

There is no answer in the book regarding the feasibility of the socialist project: "socialists don't *now* know how to replicate camping trip procedures on nationwide scale" (p. 75). The question is only knowing how to harness generosity in order to make it turn the wheels of the economy as self-interest does. The author in fact does not know if the problem is or is not insoluble, but he advances some possibilities within market socialism, only to reject them, as well to reject traditional central planning as seen in the Soviet Union and in China.

Markets, Planning and Centralization

A predatory system

"Every market, even a socialist market, is a system of predation." (p.82) So, even if the products of labour are directed to social welfare, the very basis of the system remains immoral because grounded on the market principle of self-interest. Inequalities will, accordingly, and inevitably, appear, grow and destroy the principle of community. Market socialism is not an answer to Cohen's preoccupations.

Democratic Planning?

But neither is "real socialism". The traditional central planning "is, we now know, a poor recipe for economic success, at any rate once a society has provided itself with the essentials of a modern productive system." (p.67) Since Cohen does not support any model, we cannot analyse his thesis to its full extent. Still, he does say that economists should "study noncentral planning ways of organizing [...] a socialist economy" (ibid.). And this is where the problem is raised. To Cohen, the problem is that market is *per se* immoral, while our thesis here is that planning is, *per se*, immoral, or at (the very) least it leads to immoral consequences. To Cohen, it does not matter that a market may be socialist, provided it is a market. Neither to us: being socialist is not bad. Being planned is. Let us see why.

Nicholas Vrousalis (2010, pp. 213/214) dedicates a small section of his article to show us Cohen's desire to connect democracy and the economy. According to Vrousalis, Cohen does not believe that the justification of economic planning relies on instrumentalist basis, but on moral ones. To do so, economic planning has to be nevertheless democratic. So, we are left with a democratic (and thus?) non-centralized economic planning.

But if we plan, are we not centralizing?

Cohen never develops this idea of a democratic planning, though others have tried to do so. One of the best configurations of what could be imagined as a "non-central planning" is Pat Devine's (1988) "democratic planning". The core idea is having a coordinated negotiation between planning commissions on local, regional and national levels substituting the operations of the market.

While the feasibility of this permanent negotiation scheme would certainly need to be proved on a practical level, we still have to doubt that planning and centralization are not connected by ties of necessity. Can a system be planned if it is not centralized? There are two ways of ways of answering this question, and both refute the thesis according to which democratic planning is not central planning.

The first is, and still within the framework of local, regional and national levels given by Devine, we need, for as much freedom we give to the local level, a central authority to balance local interests and ensure solidarity at the macro-level. Local wills and local interests cannot supersede the general interest in the very same way individual selfishness should not put at risk solidarity within the local community. This pyramidal system is far from not being centralized. Moreover, why are the continental and the world levels are, or at least not mentioned - if you are to design a utopia, why stop at a national level? How can Devine's model be applied to Luxembourg and to Russia? In a Russian scale, Luxembourg would be the local level. In a Luxembourgian scale, Russia would be the continent.

The second way of seeing this is to zoom in the local level. As much democratically elected a planning commission may have been, it still must hold the power of dictating how individuals may have to act. Unless human beings are transformed into perfect "caring-for-others" beings in a Cohenian style, they will have to be directed into the right goals. And even if they are perfect human beings in Cohen's style, the commissions will still have the task of *coordinating* the distribution of utilities through the population. Markets work because they fulfil two functions: "an *information* function and a *motivation* function" (Cohen, 2009, p.61). So even if the motivation issue is solved through moral excellence, markets are still needed for information reasons. So, we may conclude, democratic or not, any commission that exists to plan something has a function of a central power gathering all relevant information that would otherwise be dispersed in society. If the commission is the central power of a street, a neighbourhood, a city, a region, a country, a continent or the world, it is irrelevant.

Saying "no central planning" is a non-sense as much as saying "central planning" is an oxymoron.

II - The *feasibility* problem

Organizational models

Three ways of organizing a group

We will now create different types of organization that human groups can adopt. The first category will correspond to the participatory or "democratic" central planning that Cohen would defend. A second corresponds to a centralized type of organization, as we know in dictatorships (such as central planning regimes like the Soviet Union of the Nazi regime), armies or companies. A third is a decentralized system, where no one (person or institution, such as "commissions") holds the power to determine neither the overall destiny of the group nor the results of personal interaction. Each category has to be analysed regarding three elements: the decision-making procedures; bindingness of decisions; scope of results.

1. The *democratic centralism* model: a participatory group

The first characteristic of a democratic centralist model is that all members of the group have a say on its governance: it is *democratic*. Not only a say, but actual power of decision. That power of decision may come in variable features. It depends on how the members decided to organize themselves, which in turn depends of a plethora of different factors: the size of the group, their goal, their history, the culture in which people are embedded, etc., etc.. The decisive feature is that direct or indirect decision power exists. The group members are not only free to advise, but within the chosen framework, to effectively decide. If the group is small, then decisions may be voted by each member. If the group is very large, delegation is required, and so people will vote for representatives, gathered in commissions, who will decide for them. The bigger the group, most likely the bigger and the more complex the governance structure will be, but the basic principle is that each member as a vote on decisions for the future of the *whole* group.

And this is the second feature of democratic centralist model, meaning, the decisions taken by the group members are binding to all members: it is *centralist*. Let us see this through a simple example. Peter, Paul and Mary decided to give each ten euros to buy a birthday present to Magdalene. The fact that Peter wanted to give only five euros does not allow him to only pay five euros (unless the others agreed that he could give less because he is poorer). If the three of them reached the decision by simple vote or by negotiation (for example, Peter wanted do give five, and Mary fifteen and so they established the mean amount between the two) is irrelevant. The results of the deliberation are to be respected by all members - even if some of them do not agree with the results.

2. The *authoritarian centralism* model: a "command and obedience" group

In an authoritarian centralist model decisions are also binding for everybody, but not everybody participates in the decision process. There is a commander, or a group of commanders, who decides for the whole group. There may also be, should the group be big enough for that, a chain of command, with several levels of power.

The origins of such power may be very different and the way it is perceived (as legitimate or not) also. Commanders may base their power in their strength, in their knowledge, in their age; or may justify it by tradition, or god or something else that people believe in. The other group members may even accept to be under such a rule and, under certain circumstances, may give their advice. But in no way do they hold a power to decide. There is no voting and negotiations are rare or non-existent.

3. The decentralized model: a *catallactic* group

In a decentralized group, processes like votes do not occur, because the decentralized and unplanned nature of it is not compatible with decisions aiming to produce specific results. Accordingly, there is a multitude of small decisions affecting only parts (two or more individuals) of the group. What will be their overall result we do not (or only very difficultly will be able to) know.

Catallactics can be defined as "the order brought about by the mutual adjustment of many individual economies in a market" (Hayek, 1976, pp.108-109) which seems to be a better definition of the one given by Mises: "Catallactics is the analysis of those actions which are conducted on the basis of monetary calculation." (Mises, 1946, p.234) Hayek captures better, in its definition, the nature of catallactics (a term first used in 1831 by Richard Whateley as "science of exchanges"): what defines it is not the monetary aspect, but the nonexistence of a single plan (of an *economy*, so, a unified centre of interests and will). There are many individual plans, and the way they interact is not planned. They *mutually adjust* themselves in a dynamic, evolutionary process.

Table 1: Three organizational models and their elements

Organizational models	Decision-making procedures	Bindingness of decisions	Scope of results
Democratic	Voting, Negotiation	Binding for all	Closed
Authoritarian	Commands, Orders	Binding for all	Closed
Catallactic	Negotiation, Exchange, Adaptation	Binding for the parts	Open

Relevant dimensions to evaluate a human group

Context matters

As we have previously said, Cohen affirms that the size of the group or the nature of the camping trip do not affect its potential as a synthesizer of principles that can be applied for the wider society: "it is not only in happy contexts, but also in much less benign ones, [...] in emergencies like flood or fire" (Cohen 2009, p.54). The author is in our opinion right when saying that the same communitarian principles arise in different (and often more easily in difficult) contexts, but he is wrong when he says that context is irrelevant.

As David Schmidtz puts it "respective elements rule only over limited ranges. Ranges are topics that are mutually exclusive" (Schmidtz, 2006, p.17). There may be some principles that seem sound and fair in some contexts, but not in others. You can also imagine principles that are applicable in situations that are *apparently* very different, as Cohen did, but then you must ask yourself why, if so, they fail to answer our needs in other contexts. Just saying that you can use the same principle in this and that situation is not enough. Which characteristics unite the two situations? Which separate them?

We need to have a set of dimensions that allow us to compare different situations. We intend to develop that now.

Which dimensions count when we look into a group?

There are essentially four dimensions that we have to look at. The first is the group itself: its size, nature and duration. The second is the goal: the nature of the goal, and its commonality (if it is shared by all or not). The third is the interaction: how intense and how voluntary it is. The fourth is the cognitive dimension.

A - The group itself

In a group, the most obvious characteristic is certainly its size It is obvious that we will not interact with others in the same way when "the others" are two people, and when "the others" are two million people. Also, the type of organization needed to manage both groups will necessarily be different. Another characteristic to have in mind is the nature of the group: what unites it? Why do we call it a group? Are they family? Friends? Co-workers? Classmates? A thousand people in a factory are co-workers. There is a lot uniting them. For many hours a day they share the same space and their present and future is mutually dependent. A thousand people walking through a street are just a crowd. While the size is the same, the ties that unite these people are different - and we must take that into account. But let us look at yet another example. You and two of your best friends. Will you interact the same way if you are only going to have a drink for one hour or if you are going to go on vacations for one month? The nature of the goal (recreational) is the same, the nature and number of the group (three friends) also, but the fact that in the second case you are going to spend a long time together will force you to behave differently. In one hour only a limited amount of events may occur. In a month, you may even decide that those people are not your friends (because they showed some personality trait you never knew of them, or because they acted in an incorrect manner). In an hour, you will eventually try to make the best of the limited time, it may be an intense event. In a one month travel with two other people, you may want to avoid too many emotions (you do not want to get angry with someone you are going to spend the next thirty days) and save topics for conversation.

B - The goal

Take the same three people. If they are going to work for a year together in the same company, their goal is certainly different of the goal they will have if, instead of working in the same place, they lived a whole year sharing the same house. The duration of the interaction is the same (a year) the size of the group also (three people) and the nature of the group (they are friends). But being flatmates is not the same thing as being co-workers. Wanting to live in a clean and quiet house (or dirty and tumultuous one) is not the same thing as wanting to get your salary every month, guaranteeing that company keeps existing, etc.. There are things that you could find in common - most people will try to, both at home and at work, have a peaceful relation with others and avoid troubles - but others that are different. It is different wanting to have fun on vacations, getting your salary at work, shop in a shopping centre, see the nature in a camping trip, etc.. Other than the nature of the (general) goal, we also have to see if in more refined level the goal is substantially the same. Four people inside a car and going to visit a museum in the near town have the same substantial goal: getting to that place safe and sound.

They are in the same car and have previously agreed to visit that specific museum. On the contrary, four people in four different cars going to visit different museums in the same city have generally the same goal (getting to the desired museums safe and sound) but they do not want to visit the *same* museum. They are not completely apart in their goals, something does unite them, but they are not a community.

C - The type of interaction

The intensity of the interaction may vary according to endogenous or exogenous reasons. *Exogenous* conditions affecting it may be, for example, situations like those mentioned by Cohen: natural catastrophes cause emotional distress and tend to create tighter bonds among people. *Endogenous* conditions may result from our own lives and choices. For example, a couple has more intense interaction than two friends. A couple working in the same place has also a more intense interaction than other in which they work in different places and have different professions. The intensity does not provide straight answers, but it does give some clues. Some couples may want to be always together. Others might feel better if they only see each other at night. Some people like to bond with their neighbours and feel that they live in a community. Other people do not like nosy neighbours. In a natural catastrophe, the intensity of the interaction is due to an unfortunate event. In a party, emotional intensity comes from a common will to have some fun.

That is why we also need to understand if the interaction, and, more than that, the *cooperation* is voluntary (or if it hides a lurking conflict). In a natural catastrophe, the interaction with other people is not voluntary in the sense it is the product of an exogenous event, something we did not choose to happen. But we do cooperate on a voluntary basis: we choose to help others and we accept their help. Many times, we may choose to do something, and still we feel it is not completely voluntary in the sense that our options were so limited that we had to choose the "least awful" situation.

That is in some way what Cohen intends to say about our capitalist economies: leaving the market economy is close to impossible, it is like a casino where the gamblers did not choose to be and cannot exit: "A particular person in a market economy may face a choice of being a building laborer or a carer or starving, his set of choices being a consequence of everybody else's choices. But nobody designed things that way" (Cohen, 2009, pp.48/49). While it is difficult to exit a capitalist economy (without leaving the country), it is, nevertheless, conceivable, in the sense it does not contradict the mechanics of capitalist free market economy.

D - The cognitive dimension

In the same examples, the four friends riding the same car know other people's goal. The other four riding in different cars do not. They may not even know each other. So, their actions will only take into account what *they aim, other data* they may be in possession of (like the roads they must take to get to the museums, regulations concerning traffic or rush hours) and their *problem-solving cognitive abilities.*

Summation

We have until now created three archetypal organisation forms that would in some way correspond to the three economic models approached by Cohen: the market economy, a centrally planned economy, and a hypothetical planned but decentralized (or, as we have explained, participatory or democratic, but still centralized) economy. But the three categories are not limited to forms of organizing economies: they are to be viewed as general forms of structuring any human groups.

After doing that, we affirmed that when we defend this or that type of organization we cannot pretend it is a one-size-fits-all, as if the context did not count for something. We went from there to show a (non-exhaustive, we are sure) list of factors that affect groups.

Crossing all this data will allow us to examine Cohen camping trip's case (and three others) in a different light.

Testing the three organizational models

The camping trip group

In this case let us take four people, with different skills. They put their skills at the service of the group, sharing the results of each other's work (Harry shares the fish he caught, Sylvia the apples she found, Leslie the nuts only she knows how to crack and Morgan the perfect campsite his father prepared for him). Of course, in a recreational activity nobody is charging for anything. They feel naturally inclined to serve and be served not according to their quantitative contribution, but to their needs and their dedication to the group. Also, the group takes the decisions collectively, at each time discussing the best options, negotiating what to do and *in extremis* (should negotiation fail) taking votes and letting the majority decide.

The natural disaster survivors' group

Let us accept Cohen mention to natural disasters (2009, p.54) where according to him the socialist principles of equality and community are also visible. In this case, we do not have only four people, but a large group of many thousands of people affected by a given event. In such a dramatic situation generally people feel inclined to help others: they will help whoever they can. They will do it without asking anything in return, knowing still that most other people will also feel inclined to act likewise. The emergency management procedures are enacted, with the civil protection services articulating the fire department, the police and the military to guarantee the rescue of survivors and keep security while risks of looting and riots may exist.

The jungle trip group

Let us now imagine a different situation, joining characteristics from both previous cases. Four people with different skills take a vacation trip through an equatorial forest infested with beasts and dangerous insects, man-eating tribes and greedy explorers ready to kill whoever crosses their ways. Although having some fun is part of the trip, the four travellers want above all to get to their destination safe and sound. They depend on each other to survive, and depend of a good commander, the most experienced and skilled of the four to take the lead and coordinate them. Sometimes the majority of the group may agree with the leader, but that is not relevant:

many times they will disagree, and the leader must impose his will. It is irrelevant to know what people think about the decisions, they have to follow them.

The road

Finally, another different situation. Thousands of people going through a road. They come from different places, and go to different places. They travel in the road at different times. And they do not, generally, know each other. All they know is that they want to reach somewhere and know that, presumably, other people also have their own destination, although they are unaware of what is the specific destination of each traveller. They know that somebody has been on the road before, and that others will be on the same road after them. They themselves may also return to the same road later on. They do not have rules dictating where each person, or the whole group must go, but they have the highway code, allowing them to share a framework for interaction: "it does not matter whether we all drive on the left- or on the right-hand side of the road, so long as we all do the same. The important thing is that the rule enables us to predict other people's behaviour correctly, and this requires that it should apply to all cases - even if in a particular instance we feel it to be unjust." (Hayek, 1944, p.83).

While this general rule exists, in practice people will interact on a case-to-case basis: no one is compelled to drive faster or slower than anyone else. They will follow the speed and the way it better suits them. Sometimes they will slow down, in others they will speed up; sometimes a driver will overtake others, and sometimes he will be overtaken. There is no central power coordinating them. The group functions on an automatic, dynamic way.

Results

Having described four different situations, we have now to understand what unites and separates them. Regarding the organisational models of each one of the situations, we see that while in the first three there is a central power to plan what will the group do (respectively, the whole group; the civil protection services; and the leader), there is no such thing in the fourth case.

Simultaneously, the organisational model in the natural disaster is not democratic (although for sure Cohen's principle of community is present there). It is essentially based in centralized authority, with no consultation with the community. Although in this case people may feel attached to others, such attachment is not determinant to how the group actually works. It does share many points in common with the camping trip, as Cohen already pointed out, but it shares even more points in common with our jungle trip example. Again, it is the road example that differentiates itself from the rest of the cases.

Let us evaluate each of the four cases regarding, first, the characteristics of each group in what concerns the group itself, its goal(s), the interactions within it and the cognitive dimension.

Table 2: Summary of group's characteristics in the four discussed cases.

	Camping trip	Natural disaster	Jungle trip	Road
Group	Small size, friends, short duration	Big size, local community, short duration	Small size, friends, short duration	Big size, strangers, long duration
Goal	Common goal: recreation	Common goal: survival	Common goal: Survival	Individual, indeterminate goals
Interaction	Intense and voluntary	Intense and voluntary	Intense and involuntary	Low and voluntary
Cognitive dimension	Relevant data known	Relevant data partially known	Relevant data partially known	Unknown group size, goals, etc.

Table 3: Elements of organizational models and the four discussed cases.

	Camping trip	Natural disaster	Jungle trip	Road
Decision Process	Negotiation, Voting	Commands, Orders	Commands, Orders	Adaptation
Bindingness	For all	For all	For all	Each interaction
Results aimed	Closed (having fun) or Open (each member may do what he wishes as long as he does not menace the group)	Closed (survival)	Closed (survival)	Open (depends on each member)

Analysing the results we see that the size of the group did reveal itself less than relevant, for we have no apparent pattern: with a small group we have a democratic and an authoritarian procedure, and with a big group we have an authoritarian and a catallactic procedure.

A shared identity (friends, endangered local community), a short duration of a group with high emotional intensity and a common goal that is known to all group members, who aim at closed, specific results and take decisions binding for everyone are factors that are common to all centralist models, be they democratic or not.

On the contrary, and within the centralist models, the nature of the goal, the voluntariness of cooperation and the decision process determine the difference between democratic, participated models, or authoritarian ones.

What in conclusion we see, is that certainly the camping trip group is a democratic one. But as we said before, Cohen is wrong to think that a natural disaster group follows the same lines. In a natural disaster, the organizational model will be based in authority because the issue is pressing and not everybody has all the relevant knowledge to fulfil the required tasks. Moreover, would it be acceptable to try to make a democracy out of the road case, which follows the catallactic model? Have travellers voting on the required decisions for the group to move on? Or having them voting on representatives who would plan how the whole thing would work? That is our task in the last section.

Table 4: To which organizational model does each case correspond?

	Camping Trip	Natural disaster	Jungle trip	Road
Organisational Model	Democratic	Authoritarian	Authoritarian	Catallactic

III – The *desirability* problem

Three answers to Cohen

Approaching the moral desirability issue, three types of answers can be found, and I will try to explain all the three.

The first is actually a quasi-answer. It consists in saying that we are talking of two different realms, politics and economics, and that democracy is not a moral value, but simply a mechanism used in politics. I fear, though, that some might say that it does not fully address Cohen's question, because in some way this answer derives from our considerations on the feasibility issue.

The second answer goes to the heart of what we understand as morality and in what consists a moral being. It consists in accepting that uncertainty, imperfection, are constitutive to morality, for we are not, in the end, talking about facts, but about normative claims.

The third answer derives from the precedent. Cohen falls into a *non sequitur*: he thinks that people's choices are morally relevant: it is morally relevant that people choose, that they are aware of their choices and that they do it free of coercion. We just have to find the technology to help them to follow the good choices. *But* he ends his book (and this nobody has, to this point and to my knowledge, pointed out) not with an appeal to a social technology, but to *power*. While many would think that pretending to see society as the object of a technology as an authoritarian idea *per se* (but still, only indirectly because through an appeal to instrumental rationality) Cohen seems to go (inadvertently or not) much farther than this.

A) Quasi-answer: democracy is a political concept that is not applicable in economics

Is democracy what matters?

In its essence, a State is a centralist group: it may be democratic or it may be authoritarian, but it cannot, by definition, work in a catallactic form. Political units are, as the name says, units - and catallactics is the non-organized, non-fixed way how units peacefully interact and adapt themselves to others. So, defending a catallactics in politics would correspond to defending an anarchy. That is not our goal here. So, organizing a political unit requires a centralist model. But is it equally so in an economy? Cohen thinks so. But as we have seen, there is no one-size-fit-all organizational model. If States are naturally centralist (and they can even be so respecting people, like in democracies), we need not think that economies work or may work likewise.

"Democracy" cannot be a magic word to validate anything we want to defend. We have to *define* democracy (and eventually, defining where it is good and where it is bad). Democracy is *normally* not defined as a *simple* rule of the majority. The mere will of a majority without any respect for minorities is *normally* not accepted. Our Western-type of democracies are thus also called "liberal democracies", because it is understood that there are basic rights that no majority is allowed to trample on. So, even if the will (of the majority) the people is to kill the minority, the common understanding of democracy would not deem such attitude as "democratic".

So the fact that Cohen desires a democratic planning of the economy does not turn his model of economic planning into an immediately desirable project. Cohen does here nothing other than mixing two different things: a mechanism to achieve a good, and the good itself.

What does the economy look like?

There is a sharp difference between on the mechanisms through which a political community and an economy work, and the goals they are meant to achieve. The first has to have some degree of centralization. By definition, a political community will have some kind of pre-fixed architecture of power distribution. There will be organs which will be seen as legitimately holding some powers and not others. But not in the economy. In a political community, there are several (many times, conflicting) interests, but the belonging to the community creates some bonds between individuals. In an economy, each person works to get the salary that will allow each one to buy what he needs. Nobody knows what the others really want. I may prefer to eat rice with my meat, my neighbour may prefer to eat potatoes with his fish. It is impossible to coordinate millions of individual wishes (be they spurs of the moment or constant patterns of consumption). So how to deal with this difference between politics and economics?

So far we have showed that organizing a group of four friends is not the same thing as organizing other types of groups. In fact, it is not even the same thing as organizing a group in which, according to Cohen, we would find the same principles of equality and community, such as a group of survivors of a natural disaster. So, context matters. Following from that, we can understand that organizing a political unit and an economy are not the same thing. They can have a similar, centralized, planned, kind of organization. But *should* they?

What does the economy look like? Does it look more like a small group of friends doing a short trip somewhere and having the common voluntary goal of having some fun, or does it look more like a large group of people who do not know each other, nor other people's goals while pursuing their own ends? Our answer definitively leans towards the second case.

How can you democratically respect people's will to get to their destination if neither you nor a committee of several people can know what each and every one of the millions of members of an economy desire for their lives? Wanting to have a "democratic" planning of the economy is the same as allowing a group of thousands or millions of people voting where each person may or may not go, or, (more likely) voting to get people going all to the same places, regardless of their personal wishes and needs.

What is correct and who gets to decide

We have here what David Schmidtz calls a question of "jurisdiction": "there are two ways to agree: We agree on what is correct, or who has jurisdiction - who gets to decide. [...] Isn't it odd that our greatest successes in learning how to get together stem not from agreeing on what is correct but from agreeing to let people decide for themselves?" (Schmidtz, 2006, p.6) Who gets to decide on what is to be produced and what is to be consumed?

Planning both, even if done by a democratically elected committee, means that you take from people the right to decide what to do in their everyday live. There are central organs deciding how thousands and millions of individuals are to take intimate decisions.

Is it not curious how the most economically successful countries are not those who define how the whole economy is going to work, but those who let people decide how to lead their lives? And is it not curious that those countries are also democracies, whereas all other (even if well-intended) attempts have led to dictatorships?

B) Answer: Morality and human beings *as* moral beings

The feasibility and the desirability of an idea

Cohen defends that the feasibility and the desirability are very different things. One of the ways of seeing this is how Brennan, and also Miller, have put it: are we worried with imagining the best society we can possibly imagine, or are we worried with allowing real human people living the best life they can possibly live? Again, those are two different questions, and some philosophers, like Cohen, feel more inclined towards the first. Other philosophers, like Rawls, feel more inclined towards the second. Cohen and Rawls are addressing different questions and consequently their answers will be fundamentally different. Or, in other terms: Cohen wants to know what is the most desirable society, even if is not feasible. Rawls wants to know what is the most desirable of all the feasible societies.

My answer to this dilemma follows other paths. I would say that socialism, even in the terms (and maybe precisely because of the terms) in which Cohen puts it, is not desirable.

The City of Angels

As we have quoted before, Cohen thinks that *every person of good will* would gladly desire a society in which the principles of equality and community, like in a camping trip, are fully adopted. It is as if you were not able to desire to live in a *polis* of angels, you were a demon. But it is this angelical vision, this perfectionism, which puts at peril the very desirability of Cohen's socialism. And not only because human beings are, until this moment, with *our available social (or other) technology*, imperfect. The problem is not, essentially, because imperfection is a human characteristic. It is because imperfection is constitutive to *morality*.

A *polis* of angels is an amoral community. There are no moral issues because there are no dilemmas, there are no errors, and there are no doubts. It is when you are confronted with issues and you are not sure about the answer, because you have so many possible ways to act and even more so many ways of justifying an action, that you can think of yourself as a moral being.

Taleban and Republicans

For me, who do not believe in angels or in demons, the best possible parallel I can find is a society of machines, or robots, or programmed human beings. A society in which moral issues are instantly solved seems more like a dystopia, a Brave New World. Even if there was no central command system, like Cohen would like to imagine, even if there was no authority (or authoritarian) relations, can we actually say that we would be talking of moral, sensible, intelligent human beings?

Certainly, many of us may feel disgusted, worried, revolted when we see many of the problems that affect our world; personally, I do not like that there are Taleban; neither do I like Republicans. They represent ideas that are, totally or partially, the opposite of my own. But is it not the fact that I am able to say that something is right and something is wrong, and choose, after reflection, what I deem good over what I deem wrong, what makes me a moral being? How can we possibly know what is *right* if we cannot even *imagine* what could *wrong* be?

C) Cohen's non sequitur

People's choices: the final test

Cohen objective in *Why not Socialism* was hardly to show that socialism is feasible (or if it was, he did not make any effort in that sense). But he did try to reaffirm its alleged moral superiority. To guarantee it, socialism has not only to guarantee the principles of equality and community, but also to respect individual choices: there must be freedom of choice because it is morally relevant in rational beings.

But what to do if people do not choose to have a wholly planned economy? And after deciding to have democratically elected committees deciding what is to be produced and what, when and in which quantities is to be consumed, can we *actually speak of* personal choices?

Different concepts of society

What is our *concept* of society? The way we see them determines our political views.

Size is a factual matter: political units have thousands and millions of individuals. But, as we have seen on section II, it seems to be a less than conclusive factor. Nevertheless, we did find other characteristics that proved to be relevant. The cognitive dimension is an important one. But it is also a factual one. Cohen does agree that we have a cognitive failure that gives market economy a competitive advantage over planned economy. But other dimensions are not exclusively factual and may result or may be interpreted from a normative point of view. What is the nature of the group? Do we all have the same goal in life and society, or does each person has different notions of good that may, given some circumstances, be made mutually compatible? This is where Cohen's second principle, the principle of community, appears. He sees our large societies, composed of millions of individuals as strong communities, and not as loose ones.

Large groups are inclined to produce weaker bonds between individuals. The answer to this, in the *political* sphere, is either fabricating strong communitarian feelings (often portraying outsiders as aggressive enemies like totalitarian or theocratic regimes do) or try to decentralize power (like in democratic models). I do not believe it is a coincidence that the two examples where survival is at stake are also the examples where the authoritarian model is followed. Dictatorships tend to stress the survival of the regime, the race, the culture or the national economy to justify their actions. If we do see the urgency to make something survive, against everything and against everyone, if we do think that we are in danger, we will subscribe to authoritarian solutions.

The lurking authoritarian danger

Cohen understands that the market system answers better (on a pragmatic level, having in mind our available "social technology") to the specificities of the economy. But, because he believes that it produces unfair results, he wishes to change it. How? "Left it to itself, the capitalistic dynamic is self-sustaining, and socialists therefore need the power of organized politics to oppose it" (Cohen, 2009, pp.81-82). So, the author believes that the way to answer to the markets natural strength is political intervention.

And that is where we find a lurking authoritarian attitude: left to themselves, people will engage in market-type relationships. So, to avoid it, we need "power". Where can we, in the end, find the so-called respect for the three premises we unveiled in the beginning: that people are not morally bad, that their choices are relevant, and that it is also relevant that they are free to make their choices?

Conclusion

In this essay we have tried to answer Cohen's defence of the desirability, and eventually of the feasibility, of socialism.

We have started by explaining Cohen's argument, and tried to imagine an organization mode that would match his non-authoritarian socialism. We called it "democratic" or "democratic centralism". We created two other types of organizational modes, the authoritarian and the catallactic. We then went to analyse the multiple factors that determine groups, showing that when we look for parallels, like Cohen did, we must be attentive to avoid comparing the incomparable.

From there, we went to see how four different groups organize themselves and saw how would they fit with the dimensions and organizational models we previously created. We saw that there are some differences between the democratic and the authoritarian, but they share more between themselves than with the catallactic group. It is so because both a democratic and an authoritarian one work on a centralized way, whereas the catallactic group works on a decentralized one.

We then asked ourselves to which kinds of groups do political units such as States, and economic systems, correspond. While political organisation demands some degree of centralization, the economy works in a naturally decentralized way. The only way to avoid this, is, like Cohen suggests, using political coercion.

We are now ready to answer the questions we started with.

A centralized system (some types of centralized systems) can guarantee the respect of individual wishes. The circumstances, and the characteristics that the group may have, vary. We have seen that a political community must have decision centres. A democracy in which both political and individual liberties are guaranteed is probably the most efficient way to guarantee the respect of individual wishes. That is so because the legal and political framework of a democratic State does not determine results: it is not set from the beginning on an election which parties are to get which percentages. Small groups of people with strong bonds uniting them (like in the camping trip) may also easily entrust to the whole group the majority of the decisions, without hurting individual choices, especially because negotiation (and not mere voting) is in such case easy.

But the State can hardly answer to all of people's aspirations. Even a democratic planning with a pyramidal system (e.g. Pat Devine's) implies limits on people's life projects. For sure, the mere existence of the State already formats our lives: but the question we must put is until when does the State existence is *helping us to be free* to make (our own) choices and after which point is the State *directing* our choices? What we have asserted here is that *it is not morally acceptable for the State to centralize all major economic decisions (on production and on consumption)* because, by doing so, politics is violating the private sphere of individual preferences. Saying otherwise will mean that we conceive society as a collective force with one moral worldview, one (known by all) goal in life. Like in a camping trip or in a natural catastrophe - and not like in a road, where a multitude of individuals pursue their own ends, their own goods.

In the end, there seems to be a contradiction between Cohen's principle of community and the respect for people as moral beings. That is not so with the case of principle of equality (and even more so with the principle of equality of opportunities). Equality - even some level material equality, or socio-economic cohesion, to be accurate - is compatible with freedom of choice because in given circumstances, and within a market economy, considerable levels of material equality (or social cohesion, since absolute equality is, in practice, impossible) may be produced as an outcome of this non-planned economy. Equality of opportunities (as long as the goal is not to produce equal human beings, but human beings with equal opportunities) serves moral freedom, by giving individuals the tools to pursue their own ends. But that is not the case with the community principle, where the individual disappears by being compelled to share the same goals in life.

Cohen's "democratic" economic planning blatantly violates the status of moral beings, taking from them the right to decide on a multitude of aspects of their lives. It is not, as he proposes, just technically unfeasible for the moment. It is morally undesirable.

REFERENCES

Brennan, Jason. 2012. Is Market Society Intrinsically Repugnant?. *Journal of Business Ethics*, 106:1, pp.

Cohen, Gerald Allan. 2009. *Why not Socialism?*. Princeton: Princeton University Press.

Devine, Pat. 1988. *Democracy and economic planning: the political economy of a self- governing society*. Cambridge: Polity Press.

Hayek, Friedrich August von. 1944 [2010 edition]. *The Road to Serfdom*. New York: Routledge.

Hayek, Friedrich August von. 1976. *Law Legislation and Liberty* – Volume 2 – *The Mirage of Social Justice*. Chicago: The University of Chicago Press.

Mises, Ludwig von. 1947. *Planned Chaos*. URL: http://mises.org/books/plannedchaos.pdf (Viewed: 15 of December 2011).

Mises, Ludwig von. 1949 [2007 edition]. *Human Action*. Indianapolis: Liberty Fund.

Roemer, John E. 2010. "Jerry Cohen's *Why Not Socialism?* Some Thoughts". *Journal of Ethics*, 14, pp.255-262.

Schmidtz, David. 2006. Elements of Justice. New York: Cambridge University Press.

Singer, Peter. 1982. "The Right to be Rich or to be Poor", in J. Paul (ed.), *Reading Nozick*. Oxford: Basil Blackwell.

Vrousalis, Nicholas, 2010. "G. A. Cohen's Vision of Socialism". *Journal of Ethics*, 14 pp.185-216.

Wolff, Jonathan. 1991. *Robert Nozick: Property, Justice and the Minimal State* Oxford: Basil Blackwell.